WOOL STITCHERY

By the Author

EXAMPLES OF WOOL STITCHERY

WOOL STITCHERY

Originally Entitled *Embroidery in Wools*

BY

OSMA GALLINGER TOD

GRAMERCY PUBLISHING COMPANY · NEW YORK

To My Mother
whose expression of the beautiful developed the author's
desire for creative home-making

PREFACE

A VERY wise woman has said that the home should be the centre but not the circumference of the affections. It is the author's desire to extend beyond her own home centre, to share with others, the joys she has experienced in brightening the home in numerous ways available to every woman. Touches here and there of gay and harmonious colours, and bits of design enlivening otherwise blank surfaces, combine to create an atmosphere expressive of that love of the home and pleasure in adorning it that plays so large a part in the life of the average woman. To make more widely available the writer's accumulated store of knowledge of yarns and their many uses in decorating the home, this little book is offered. It is the author's hope, too, that some of her own joy in handling the lovely yarns so entrancing in colour and texture, some of her satisfaction in creating articles of home use at once original and beautiful, and some of the solace that comes in turning away from household cares or from the fatigue of social duties, to a carefree employment of the hands with materials that delight the sense of sight and of touch, may be experienced by others.

OSMA GALLINGER TOD

The bearded dwarf, shadowed by his mushroom, all embroidered in earth tones with white accents, and, of course, a snowy wool beard.

Courtesy of Lily Mills

CONTENTS

ILLUSTRATIONS

COLOUR

ILLUSTRATIONS

WOOL STITCHERY

WOOL STITCHERY

CHAPTER I

THE IMPORTANCE OF WOOL

HAVE you ever realized the important part wool plays in the life of mankind? Have you ever paused to trace through its fascinating history this important textile whose shining strands, woven into the fabric of the centuries, gleam in the mythological tale ʻ of the Argonauts and engage the serious attention of modern legislatures? Significant, indeed, it is that this famous expedition of the ancient Greeks should have been in search of the Golden Fleece; for down through the ages men have sought eagerly to find or to evolve more priceless breeds of sheep with their costlier grades of wool. As Medea aided the Argonaut Jason in winning and bearing away home to Greece from Colchis strand the Golden Fleece, so through the centuries women have aided men in transmuting the fibres of the sheep's natural coat into glossy yarns and fabrics of increasing worth and beauty.

Much we owe to the gentle sheep, whow as man's first domesticated animal, bearing on his back potential warmth for the world's comfort. For thousands of years he has submitted to the many changes in the process of selective breeding; for our woolly sheep of

PLATE I

By embroidering with wool on the warp threads of a loom, one can create fabulous transparencies and hangings, akin to tapestry. This bird, "the Roc," created by Bertha Anderson, is in red, purple, gold and orange wool with highlights of colour in ribbon. Use heavy tapestry needles and pass wool in and out of the taut warp threads.

to-day has been gradually developed from a long-haired sheep with soft down next to his skin. Wool has been of greater use to us than any other fibre. Substitutes have been found for cotton, flax and silk; but nothing has yet been discovered or invented that has those qualities of adaptability, durability, warmth, and softness of texture that make wool indeed a veritable golden fleece.

Sheep are now raised in herds of thousands in every land; but pastoral legends present a more poetic picture of the shepherd and his flock outlined against green hillsides under blue Asiatic skies. Here there was a tribal pride in owning fine breeds, and a pure white wool-bearing sheep is said to have been raised by the Arabs. More poetic, too, than mass production in the factories of to-day is the ancient domestic scene of the women of the household straightening and spinning the wollen fibres by hand, and later busily plying the shuttle to "weave them into a pattern rare." Egypt, Babylonia, and Greece had their woven woollen tunics, and in Roman times every large household had its weaving establishment directed by the women. With wool they ornamented the elaborately designed textures embellishing the temples of the gods and the palaces of royalty. The finest wool-bearing sheep of to-day are, indirectly, descendants of Roman breeds, and we find sheep raising a part of the life of the early Britons, who were using wool for their clothing even before the Roman conquest.

Nations carefully guarded their fine wool-producing sheep, but in unforeseen ways the breeds travelled. Sometimes sheep were stolen and smuggled across the boundaries of adjacent nations. There is an interesting story told of the Merino strain, famous for their very heavy growth of wool. A Spanish shepherd, Columbino, produced this breed in A.D. 100 by crossing some Tarentine ewes with African rams. But the Spanish sovereign, proud of his acquisition, soon made so many gifts of fine examples to other rulers that the Merino travelled to almost every country in the world. By the fifteenth century Spain had lost to England her supremacy in the growing of wool, and even to-day the British Empire, in her dominion, Australia, continues to lead in quantity production. There are now over three dozen distinct breeds of sheep in Britain, and of all the breeds in the United States of America, most of them have been imported from Great Britain.

In the weaving industry, too, England came even before the beginning of the modern age to leading position. A real inspiration was given to British industry by immigrant Flemish weavers, who, driven from Flanders by floods at the time of William the Conqueror, started several weaving guilds. Encouraged by succeeding kings and stimulated by various inventions, the woollen industry grew to huge proportions. The story goes that a woman helped a great deal in establishing the industry. This woman was Philippa, wife of Edward III, who, being herself a Netherlander, was only too eager to have skilled wool-workers brought over from the Continent. One of the most successful guilds was started in the town of Worstead, and here was produced the very finest of woollen fabrics that came to be known as worsteds. Some historians even say that the town's name was really "Woolstead," the stead, or place, for making wools. At any rate, the name "Worstead" came to be applied not only to fine woollen cloths but also to the fine, soft, lightly twisted woollen yarns with which we crochet, knit, and embroider.

PLATE II
A jacket creation of ecru with effective seams and
edges in sand and brown
Designed by Eve Peri

As we develop our unique and lovely creations from many shades of soft coloured yarn, it is a pleasure to know not only the history of the woollen industry but also the processes that each strand of wool undergoes before it passes through our nimble fingers. To make

yarn, the wool, first sheared from the sheep's back
(in these days by machinery), is then scoured and
oiled preparatory to carding. The woollen fibres are
straightened out in the carding process by running
them through cylinders having wire spikes, and finally
the filaments are twisted into strands of yarn on a
spinning frame.

There are so many kinds of woollen yarns available
that one wonders how the great variety is secured—all
from much the same kind of wool coming from the backs
of sheep. Yarns are made different by their dyeing and
finishing. They may be rendered glossy, lustrous, or
fluffy by various kinds of brushing; or closer and less
woolly by pressing and shearing. Fancy yarns are made
by twisting in among the woollen fibres strands of silk,
or woollen strands of other colours. Every conceivable
variety of colour and texture and an astonishing wealth
of combinations, produced by the intricate machinery
of to-day, impel one, by their surpassing loveliness, to
seek new ways of using this most seductive material;
and one turns naturally to new embroidery stitches
suitable for use on objects at once decorative and
useful in the home, and for the embellishment of
personal attire.

CHAPTER II

THE ROLE OF WOOLCRAFT

PLATE III
Woolcraft accents on table linens

EVERY woman wants her home to be as thoroughly cheerful and liveable as any; not necessarily as expensive, but having an equally charming atmosphere. It is possible for you to give to your home this coveted quality, to make it the most restful place imaginable. Give free reign to your particular preference for certain forms and colours, and work these out with intelligence. A home is like a painting, said to be never finished by the artist, needing always one last touch to bring out its greater beauty.

Making your home a masterpiece is a thrilling task, achieved fascinatingly step by step. With the help of modern literature on decoration, colour schemes may be selected, harmonious objects chosen, and these grouped artistically. Perhaps most enjoyable of all is the making up of the fabrics that soften the lines of the room; the development of each textile object into something of loveliness; its adornment with colour to bring it into closer relationship with the rest of the room; and the finishing of its edges with smart borders. To describe some of the many beautiful ways of using wool as a textile trimming is the province of this book.

Woollen yarns seem, because of their softness of texture and range of colour, to belong also to the clinging fabrics of which a woman's house gowns are made. It is possible for the individual to do much with her own skill in creating robes appropriate in colour to her background. How gratifying for the hostess to feel that her apparel is in keeping with her home! Woollen embroideries are of great help in beautifying simple and uninteresting clothes; and the smartest of new creations can be worked out by hand by using woollen stitches in making up a pattern.

THE PLEASURE OF WORKING WITH YARN. One could not hope to find a more agreeable material to work with than wool. Textures velvety, silky, soft as fur, delight the touch and produce a mood that is likely to express itself in beautiful form. This work may be done with crochet-hook or needle. The pliability of the strands of yarn and their ease of handling make it possible to cover spaces quickly, and one is delighted to watch the progress of a design as it grows from the first simple steps to ever more colourful unfolding.

While many of us love to embroider, we cannot start a pretentious piece of fine needlework with any assurance of finishing it soon, and it is just here that woolwork fills the need for an engaging home handicraft that will produce practical things with ease. For those

PLATE IV
The Insect. Iridescent blues and turquoise with green in a few
simple stitches on a natural background create a stunning
stained glass effect.
Designed by Pera Lee for Yarn and Design Studio, Coral Gables, Florida

whose eyesight has been overtaxed with fine embroidery, woolcraft gives a ready means of continuing the same type of handiwork with less strain upon the eyes. It is work one may tuck into the odd moments between the hours of other home duties, a truly constructive recreation that will make a garden of a life of loneliness, put gay notes into days that are drab, and suggest colourful motives for fingers that unconsciously have grown idle.

WOOLCRAFT IS ECONOMICAL. Woollen embroidery is most practical from the standpoint of economy. With reliable directions and a good design one can rival expensive articles. A bit of fabric, a ball of wool, a little thought and patience—these combine to produce creations giving more aesthetic pleasure than things purchased at store counters. Expensive purchasing can never take the place of your own conscientious touch. You will find that a knowledge of woolcraft is like an investment yielding rich returns. Every object made gives the ability to make another, and there is always an inviting stitch just around the corner, a tool for eager fingers to use. The most ordinary of materials, as burlap, unbleached muslin, or even oilcloth become amazingly smart when dressed up with stitches in vari-coloured yarns.

COMBINING WOOLS IS A CREATIVE ART. Woolcraft develops one's ability to blend colours artistically. Like the subtly suggested tones on an artist's palette, the colours of woollen yarn tempt one into trying new combinations. Lovely forms develop until there is complete joy in transferring Nature's colour harmonies to fabrics. The endless array of colours in old-fashioned gardens, the gorgeous mosaic on a butterfly's wing, the rich glory of an autumn landscape, the passing colours in the sunset sky—all give us patterns and colours to duplicate with delicate shades of wool.

As we give this expression to the creative impulse, our homes become more than mere shelters. They are evidences of our skill and taste, and we find ourselves living more fully in suitable backgrounds; while our friends come to spend with us bright congenial hours, receiving, perhaps, new ideas and the urge to use them for the enlivening of their own homes.

CHAPTER III

BRIGHT-COLOURED woollen seams add charm to plain fabrics employed in the home and produce a textural effect that never appears in printed or machine-embroidered goods. Decorative touches of colour are, after all, the *sine qua non* of the attractive home, drawing the eye like the gorgeous spot of flame on a bird wing. Colour notes serve also to pull several different textiles into closer relationship, thus preserving an essential harmony.

Uninteresting lengths of fabric often need the woollen seam to enliven them. If your window draperies are monotonous because of covering a large area, try breaking them up with embroidered or crocheted seams of a delicately contrasting wool—and this may be done either along their length or width. A couch cover of plain monk's cloth, poplin, linen, or homespun may have the same treatment, and the colour of the seams acts as a link to relate the cover to the rest of the room. Wall hangings, piano scarves, chair backs, pillows—may all make use of the woollen seam in having coloured borders of another tone attached to their edges. When, in the interests of economy, narrow widths of material are used, woollen seams may be effectively employed to combine the cut pieces into an attractive whole.

Woollen seams also play a large part in adding that smart touch to jackets, dressing robes, and gowns. A

PLATE V

Embroidered wool dolls (the White Rabbit, the King, and
the Mad Hatter from *Alice in Wonderland*) made into
charming soft toys by the use of simple seam and edge
stitches. [Description on page 24.]

colourful seam-line following the curves of the body
gives distinction to the contour. The parts of a dress
may be joined entirely by seams of a becoming colour.
It is most entertaining to work out these effects.
Ordinary patterns are used, the cloth is cut out in the
usual way, but instead of the customary needle-and-
thread seam, a row of crochet is added to the edge of
each piece, and the crocheted edges of adjacent pieces
are joined with overcasting stitches in wool. A *robe
d'intérieure* is shown in Plate I, page 2, made of a
soft woollen fabric called "Albatross," with seams of
crocheted wool. It is of orchid colour with seams of
purple and rose, and a decorative sleeve motif embroidered with simple woollen stitches in tones of pale
and deep purple, rose, and carmine. A charming house
jacket in Plate II, page 5, is made of delicate beige
homespun, joined with wide seams combining tan and
deep brown.

A SIMPLE SEAM STITCH (Fig. 1). A simple but useful
seam is shown in Fig. 1. The two edges to be joined are
placed flat together, right sides out, and held in the left
hand. The needle of wool is inserted at A, and a stitch
taken under the material at the left side, $\frac{3}{16}$ in. or more
from the edge, as at B; then into the right edge, and
so on, alternating from side to side. When the stitching
is finished, the edges are opened out and the seam
pressed flat. If the stitches are taken a little farther
apart, they appear as a diagonal joining, as at C.

These simple stitches combine into a most useful
seam to enliven the curtains of breakfast room, dining-
room, kitchenette and nursery, where an atmosphere of
cheer is essential and handiwork adds interest and charm.
The colour of the wool used should be a contrasting

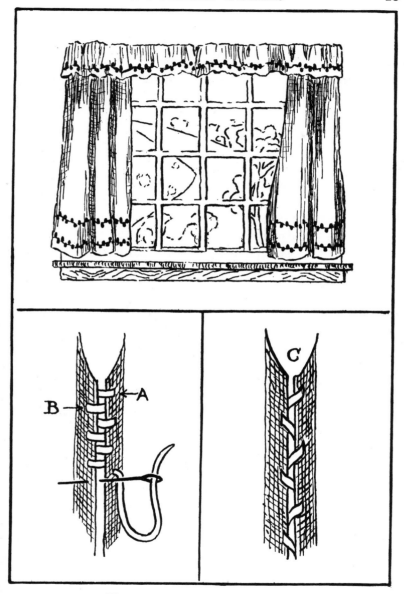

FIG. 1. SIMPLE SEAM STITCH

colour to the border applied or a deeper shade of the same colour, so that the decorative stitching will show. The seam may be applied in several horizontal lines along a curtain, as shown in the illustration (Fig. 1), with the addition of other woollen stitches at either side of the seam if desired. Small pieces of different material may be put together in this way to make a useful length of fabric. Cleverly combined stripes are always smart. The modern vogue for several shades of a colour in series, such as a drapery with bands of pale blue, medium blue, and very deep blue, recurring again and again in groups of three successive bands, may be imitated at the lower portion of a curtain by joining different coloured bands with woollen seam stitches.

This seam may be used to lengthen children's dresses with new hems, to add pretty borders to bags, and to give a touch of smartness to neck scarves by stitching a border of accenting colour at each end.

KNOTTED SEAM STITCH (Fig. 2). The second seam stitch, Fig. 2, is a zigzag knotted stitch. It is excellent for attaching borders to table-runners, wall-hangings, and pillows, and it may have a similar use to Stitch No. 1 in joining the separate lengths of window draperies. Nothing could be more attractive and colourful than this little stitch applied between the yoke and the main part of a child's dress, and between the cuffs and sleeves. By virtue of its very definite character the stitch may be used as a decorative finish for objects in the living room or hall. An intimate grouping adopting it as a trimming is shown in the illustration (Fig. 2), where a wool-embroidered flower panel of spun silk of a loose weave is edged with a border of a slightly

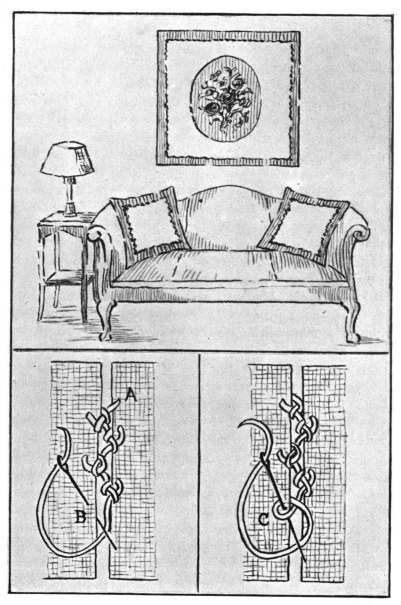

FIG. 2. KNOTTED SEAM STITCH

deeper shade than the main colour, joined by woollen
stitches in colour harmony. The pillows are made to
correspond, and no other ornament seems necessary.
The stitch is really composed of two successive button-
hole stitches. Baste the two edges to be joined to a
piece of smooth wrapping paper with about $\frac{1}{4}$ in. space
between them. Insert the needle in the upper edge of
the right piece, as shown in Fig. 2, A. Carry thread
across to left piece, insert needle about $\frac{3}{16}$ in. from edge,
and bring it out above the woollen strand, as shown
at B. Now take a little button-hole stitch into the loop
just made, as shown at C, bring the needle out above
the strand, and tighten into a knot. For next stitch on
other side, throw strand under the needle and take a
stitch similar to that shown at B, $\frac{1}{4}$ in. to $\frac{1}{2}$ in. below
the stitch just made at C. Finish the stitch with a knot
as at C. Continue these knot stitches, alternating from
side to side.

DECORATIVE SEAMS (Fig. 3). An unusually decorative
stitch is shown in Fig. 3, in the drawing at the left.
This is splendid when worked with a contrasting colour
of wool between the vertical or horizontal panels of a
studio curtain. If used vertically it forms long, colourful
lines, making the window appear higher; and if used
to join horizontal strips, it forms interesting bands,
giving the window an appearance of greater breadth.
When the stitch is employed to attach borders to
doilies, table-covers, and pillows, as illustrated, very
little other trimming is necessary.

Each group of stitches is nothing more than three
button-hole stitches placed side by side. Arrange the
two pieces to be joined parallel to each other, and for
greater convenience baste to smooth paper. The needle,

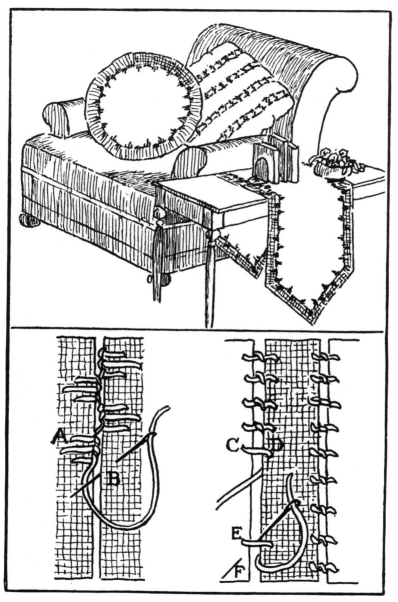

FIG. 3. DECORATIVE SEAMS

coming out in Fig. 3, *A*, takes a button-hole stitch
$\frac{1}{4}$ in. long, then a button-hole stitch $\frac{3}{8}$ in. to $\frac{1}{2}$ in. long,
and a third one $\frac{1}{4}$ in. long. The needle and yarn now
goes to the opposite side, *B*, a trifle below the last stitch
taken, and takes three similar stitches. Alternate with
groups of three stitches from side to side.

Fancy woollen seams may be used to insert a band
in an expanse of otherwise monotonous colour. Fig. 3
shows how this is done with stitches at either side. A
strip of colour between the edge and main part of a table-
runner, a band of coloured loveliness at the base of
portières, another material inserted in the sleeve of a
dress—all make for charm and individuality. The
square pillow in the illustration is made of strips of felt
put together with this seam stitch.

Arrange the pieces to be joined side by side, basted
to paper if necessary. The stitch enters the material
at the 'left, as in Fig. 3, *C*, crosses the gap, enters at
the opposite side at *D*, and comes out below stitch.
To make the twisted bar, insert needle under the
stitch from above, as shown at *E*, and bring it out
through the material at the left side, as shown at *F*.
This point, *F*, is $\frac{3}{8}$ in. to $\frac{1}{2}$ in. below the last stitch.
Continue from *F* to make the next stitch.

OPENWORK SEAM (Fig. 4). So often we keep on
purchasing the commercial article for our homes, and
continue to wonder why they have that commonplace
appearance. However, we can easily alter this with
just a little ingenuity in applying a bit of embroidery
or woolcraft stitchery here and there. For instance,
in the hall curtains shown (of pale peach theatrical
gauze or net), a border of deep coral was added with an
openwork seam of wool in self tone, coral being the

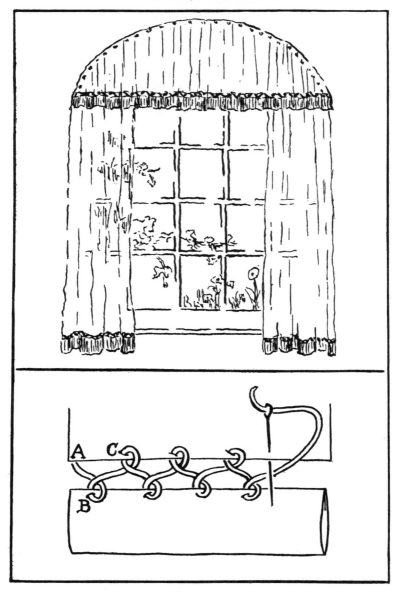

FIG. 4. OPENWORK SEAM STITCH

tone employed elsewhere in the hall. Openwork seams
are practical to use in panels, pillows, bedspreads, and
draperies; while for personal attire they are useful to
add bias bindings to dresses, borders to collars, decorative ends to scarves, etc.

The openwork seam is one of the easiest of woollen
seam stitches. The needle starts from underneath the
main material as shown in Fig. 4, A, and crosses diagonally over to B, entering the goods about $\frac{1}{8}$ in. from the
edge. The yarn, coming out underneath point B, crosses
above strand AB, and proceeds diagonally to the
other side to point C. From here it continues stitching
from side to side, always crossing above the last
diagonal stitch taken.

CROCHETED SEAMS (Fig. 5). The four preceding
diagrams show seam stitches made with needle and wool,
but the crocheted seams shown here, executed in contrasting or harmonizing colours, make most effective
joinings. In the illustration (Fig. 5) ornamental ends
were attached to plain monk's cloth *portières* with
wide crocheted seams of a bright, beautiful colour.
Crocheted seams are stunning in *négligés* of soft
clinging cotton or woollen cloth, as shown in Plate I.
Sport dresses and blouses acquire that smart look when
their contours are strengthened with woollen seam-lines.

Fold under each edge to be joined $\frac{3}{16}$ in. or more,
and crease. Basting is unnecessary; the crocheting
holds the edge in. On each edge to be joined a border
of single crochet is worked, taking two chain stitches
between each two fastening stitches, so that a space
of about $\frac{1}{4}$ in. is left, as shown in Fig. 5, A. For every
stitch insert the hook $\frac{1}{4}$ in. or more down into the cloth,
then take two more chain stitches, as shown at B. Now

FIG. 5. CROCHETED SEAMS

insert the hook into cloth as at C, and draw loop D through the cloth. Throw yarn across hook as at E, and bring wool through loops B and D as shown at F. Continue crocheting all along the folded-down edge until covered.

Along one of the edges thus crocheted, put a solid row of crochet in a smartly contrasting colour, using either plain, double or treble crochet, as at G and H. To do this take a stitch into every deep stitch of row preceding, as at G, and also between each two stitches, around the chain stitching, as at H. Now place the edge of material having only the single edge, opposite this edge having the solid crochet added, and sew them together with needle and wool, using over-and-over stitches with one of the colours of wool, as shown in Fig. 5, I. The solid crochet, being of another colour, is thus framed between the two simply crocheted edges as shown at J. If double or treble crochet is used, the seam will be wider and more effective.

Embroidery and crochet stitches can be cleverly adapted to the making of soft toys for the children, as well as adding colour to their clothes. In fact, if a doll design is pencilled on unbleached muslin, the children themselves will find fascination and delight in using bright coloured yarns to outline the figures and add decorative motifs. The *Alice in Wonderland* dolls shown in Plate V are embroidered in gay tones of wool on plain muslin, using many of the crewel stitches given in this book. The hearts, stars and circles are accented by outlining them in contrasting colours with any of the stitches shown in Chapter VI and Figure 11, page 48. The dolls themselves, stuffed with cotton batting, are closed at their edges by crochet stitches or the woollen edges illustrated in Chapter IV.

CROCHETED CHAIN INSERTIONS (Fig. 6). A very

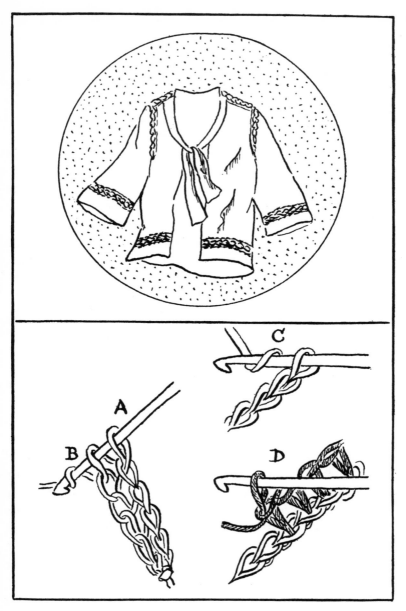

FIG. 6. CROCHETED CHAIN INSERTIONS

pretty way of enlarging a sweater is to remove the sleeves, then crochet an entirely separate chain of wool in contrasting colour, press flat, and sew this in between the sleeves and the body of the sweater. Dresses may be handled in the same way, inserting the crocheted chains at the shoulders, at the cuffs, or along any good pattern lines. A dress lacking in smart appeal may be taken apart and have crocheted chains added in the manner of Fig. 6. On pillows or portierres woollen chains make effective designs when appliquéd along a stamped pattern. They appear much like crewel work. Crochet chains of many colours, and stitch them along the pattern lines, either by hand or with the sewing machine.

A double chain of some width is shown in Fig. 6, A. Begin the chain with two chain stitches and insert the hook in the loop of the first chain stitch. Now throw the wool over the hook and pull it through the two loops, as shown at B. To continue, put the hook in the left part of the stitch just made, throw over, pull through, throw over again and pull through the two loops, etc. Press chain flat with a hot iron under a damp cloth, and sew this chain seam with wool and needle in between the sweater parts.

Another chain insertion, wider, and having two colours, is shown at D. Crochet a single chain with the first colour, as at C, then crochet a single or double crochet stitch into the openings at one side of the chain, as at D. This may be of another colour. Press flat and insert. These chains may be made any width. They are stunning additions to bags, alternating material with crocheted chain, etc. Small pieces of expensive material may be salvaged by inserting them in fabrics, and covering the joinings with such bands of crochet.

CHAPTER IV

WOOLLEN edges are smart, colourful, and easy to execute. They do for plain fabrics what clever seasoning does for simple foods, adding just that touch of personal equation that saves them from insipidity. When one is eager to add a touch of freshness and colour to the home, woollen edges matching the design in a fabric give it distinction and character. Even a drab-looking living-room set of last year may have a drastic springtime renovation by subjecting it to a good tubbing and the versatile dye-bath, and applying to it one's skill in woolcraft. Nosegays very simply embroidered in cross-stitch or chain-stitch, with edges of wool to match, make these recreated fabrics echoing colour notes to the flowers in the garden seen through the window.

You will find woollen edges adaptable at some time to every room in the home. In the kitchen, curtains and doilies of gingham, dyed muslin, glass towelling, and printed cotton, are effectively made up by edging with wool. In the dining-room we apply woollen edges to net, theatrical gauze, monk's cloth, casement cloth, crêpe, etc.; in the bedroom, to scrim, muslin, organdie, gingham, linen, and silk mesh materials; and in the living room, to heavy fabrics such as monk's cloth, casement cloth, burlap, tapestry cloth, antique cloth, and coarse linens. A list of materials is given in the last chapter of this book, with suggestions of wools and effective colour schemes to use.

PLATE VI

A bright coloured wall hanging of sunflowers
in an embroidered flower pot. Description on
page 38.

Courtesy of Lily Mills

Woollen edges are necessary to save the frayed edges of things—our portierres, our pillows, even our rugs. I have taken a hooked rug that had a design too interesting to permit of its being discarded, and entirely changed its worn look by crocheting a band of harmonizing colour around the edge.

Woollen edges are smart for use on one's attire. Shopping bags, envelope purses, scarves and sleeves with designs and edges in wool are appropriate for any season of the year. Felt, homespun and silk hats are greatly improved by a crocheted or stitched edge, and dresses and jackets acquire chic with every added touch of coloured yarn.

Everyone has access to the many crocheted edges described in books on crochet, and their charming results are apparent in the edges shown in Plates II, IV, XII, and XIII of this book. In this chapter we shall give also some of the many delightful edges that can be made with needle and wool. These use much less and are perhaps more interesting because there is a greater variety to choose from.

ROLLED EDGES (Fig. 7). Rolled edges are among the most useful of borders. They are firm and durable, and their rounded quality is most attractive. The stitches are taken over closely rolled edges; basting is usually unnecessary as the edges are rolled over with the left hand while the right hand does the stitching.

The first rolled stitch, Fig. 7, A to D, is nothing more than a cross-stitch at the edge of the material, and is used for articles having cross-stitch motives. Roll over the edge of the material with the left hand, making a roll $\frac{3}{16}$ in. (or more) thick. Start stitching as at A, and take over-and-over stitches with the right hand, as

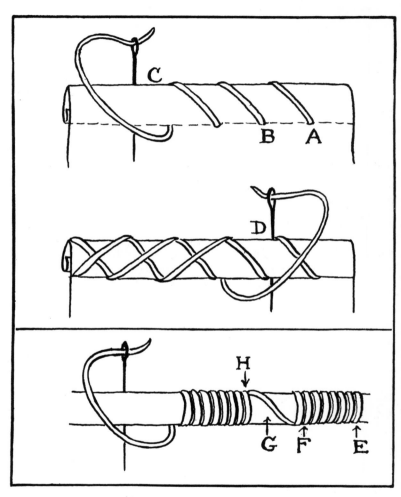

FIG. 7. ROLLED EDGES

FIG. 7A. FLOWER-POT COVER AND RUNNERS
WITH ROLLED EDGES

far apart from *A* to *B* as the hem is wide, inserting the
needle vertically as at *C*. Go all around the edge in
this way. Now reverse and stitch back with over-and-
over stitches, inserting the needle vertically in the same
holes, as shown at *D*. This forms a cross-stitch. The
rolled edge may turn over to the right side or to the
wrong side of the material, as preferred.

The material for the second rolled edge, Fig. 7, *E* to *H*,
is rolled tightly in the left hand. Start the wool at the
inside edge of the roll, at *E*, the roll for this edge
generally being taken on the right or upper side. Take
eight or ten stitches around the roll close together as
at *E* to *F*, then skip a space as at *G*, and follow with the
same number of close stitches again. This is a simple,
effective, and easy stitch.

How attractive these woollen borders make a porch
set of monk's cloth or burlap, as shown in the frontispiece! Doilies of rather coarse linen with rolled
borders are just the thing for garden tea service. In
the illustration (Fig. 7A), is shown a flower-pot cover
matching a porch set of monk's cloth or matting. First,
a cardboard cylinder is made, large enough to cover
the flower pot, by sewing ends of flexible cardboard
together. On a piece of cloth long enough to go around
this cylinder, a design is embroidered in chain- or cross-
stitch. The cloth is then sewn or pasted around the
cardboard cylinder. Waste baskets made in the same
way are splendid for the summer porch.

BUTTON-HOLE VARIATIONS (Fig. 8). Some interesting variations of the button-hole stitch are shown in
Fig. 8. The edges may be turned under in hem form
and basted, or just one turn taken, as shown at *A*. This
may be basted down for ease in working. The curtains

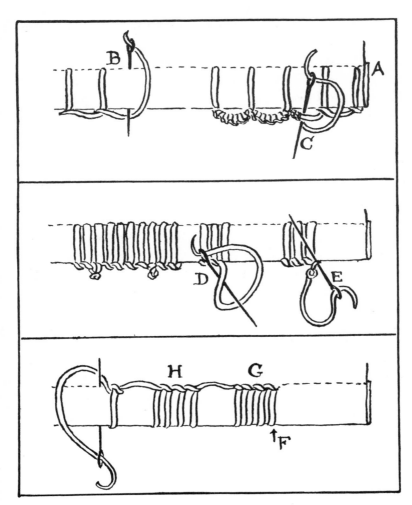

FIG. 8. BUTTON-HOLE VARIATIONS

shown, having such a simple dignity, may be edged with any of the following stitches, and smart little sprays of cross-stitched flowers in a colour to match the edging are used for ornament.

1. The stitch, A to C, is rather decorative and suitable for fabrics in living-room and dining-room. The first time around the edge, plain button-holing is used with stitches $\frac{1}{4}$ in. to $\frac{3}{8}$ in. from the edge, and the same distance apart, as at B. The second time around, with the same or a contrasting colour of wool, the lower, or loop part of the first stitch is covered with from five to ten close button-hole stitches, as at C. Continue from loop to loop.

2. The second stitch, D to E, is also nothing more nor less than that versatile stitch, button-holing, with the added attraction that at every fifth stitch there is a camouflage picot. Make the picot as follows: at the finish of the fifth stitch make a knot close to the edge, as at D; then insert the needle back into the base of the stitch, as at E; the yarn is now ready to begin on the next plain button-hole stitch.

3. The third stitch, F to H, is another variety of the button-hole stitch, this time turned upside down, and with the stitched edge $\frac{1}{4}$ in. or more inside the edge of the material. Turn the diagram upside down to see the direction of the stitch. The needle comes out at F, takes several button-hole stitches $\frac{1}{4}$ in. from the edge, as at G, then skips a space and takes several more, as at H. A second colour may be used in the spaces.

EDGES IN TWO COLOURS (Fig. 9). The first stitch in Fig. 9 is a regularly repeated button-hole stitch using two colours of wool. One colour is used the first time around the edge; and the other colour the second time. Turn

Fig. 8a. Draperies with Button-hole Edges

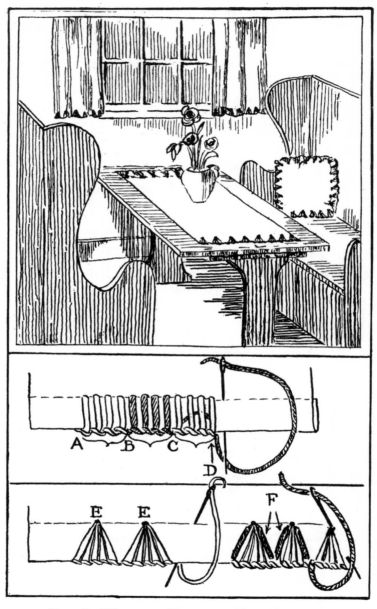

FIG. 9. WOOLLEN EDGES IN TWO COLOURS

the edge of the material under once, not twice as for a hem, although a hemmed edge may of course be covered. Bring the first needle of wool out at *A*, and take four or five button-hole stitches. At *B* skip a distance and bring yarn out at *C*. Take four more stitches, skip space, etc., all around edge. Now take the second colour of yarn, bring it out from underneath at *B*, and take four button-hole stitches in space left by first strand and over it, from *B* to *C*. Take a concealed fastening stitch through wool in back of goods between *C* and *D*, as shown by dotted line, and bring wool out at *D*, ready to take next group of stitches. Great liberty may be taken with button-hole stitches, sometimes using only one colour and leaving an open space between groups of stitches, sometimes using several colours in succession to make a rainbow border, each colour making a group of three or four stitches.

The second stitch is made with two colours or two shades of the same colour, using the darker as the outline. Fold under material. Take the lighter of the two colours, and with points *E* as guides, placed $\frac{1}{4}$ in. to $\frac{1}{2}$ in. apart, and the same distance from edge, work button-hole stitches in outgoing rays, inserting the needle in the same hole five or six times, and carrying the stitches along adjacently at the bottom. At the sixth stitch start in the next hole to the right as shown. When this radiating border has been finished all around, take the darker wool and outline the sections with back stitches from inside points to outer margin points, as shown at *F*. The radiating stitch alone, without a second colour, is also most serviceable.

Borders such as these, showing up so plainly, are excellent for bright, cheery colour notes in sun parlour, children's rooms, and in dark halls. In the breakfast nook shown, the radiating stitch was used, worked in pale green wool with accents of bright green on a soft yellow-cream background. Plate VI, page 28 shows sunflowers with radiating yellow and gold petals around black wool centers outlined in red. The petal points are held down by tiny stitches at their ends.

CHAPTER V

A STITCH OF UNIQUE CHARM

THERE are universal favourites among fancy-work
stitches just as there are among people. Quite capable
of belonging to a select group of stitches, both practical and popular, is this little square woven medallion
of Egyptian origin, shown in Fig. 10.

Exceedingly fascinating in execution and decorative
in effect, its roles are many. It is popular on bags;
it makes a fine finish for a flat pocketbook or card
case; it trims the ends of scarves; it may be worked
into effective medallions for hats; and it is adorable on
the collars and cuffs of woollen dresses. It is also of
great use in the home. Around the edges of table-
cloths or parlour scarves, it forms a splendid finish. For
the edges of curtains it is unrivalled, as shown in the
delicate effectiveness of Plate VII, page 40. By the
use of this stitch alone you may decorate the portierres,
draperies, and table scarves in your living-room, and
there is no more interesting finish for the fabrics of any
room, especially the guest-room. As the stitch resem-
bles cross-stitch it may be used wherever the latter is
appropriate, for instance, to make little figure borders
at the ends of towels or to adorn children's dresses. It
is not a hard stitch to work, and as your skill grows
in its execution, it will become an indispensable aid to
your textile creations.

The four corners of the stitch form a square just as
in cross-stitch, and for this reason it is easily applied to

PLATE VII

When sunshine filters through gauze curtains, borders
of bright woollen yarns are outlined in colourful
beauty

Designed by George E. Fowler

check materials, as shown by the borders at the bottom of Fig. 10. At K, several rows of the stitch are embroidered alternately, covering up squares on a check pattern. The rows may be worked in diagonal lines, as at L. At M, five little squares are ingeniously put together to form a larger medallion, and this is the stitch used for the edges of the net draperies in Plate VII. The stitch is equally effective used on plain materials, since it forms attractive squares.

As you consult the diagrams necessary to explain the method of working, go slowly, step by step, and the stitch will unfold clearly. On a trial piece of material execute a sample stitch. Mark four little dots on the cloth forming a square, as shown in Fig. 10, A, and this square should be about $\frac{3}{8}$ in. for fine wools, $\frac{1}{2}$ in. for thicker wools. If check materials are used, the points are already marked. Start with a needle of yarn coming out at upper right corner. Go to the lower right corner, as shown at A, and here take a buttonhole stitch with the needle, pointing to the centre of the square and brought over the yarn. This stitch is a small one—just enough to hold the yarn at the corner—taking up $\frac{1}{16}$ in. of material. Now go to the lower left corner, as at B, and take the same kind of stitch. Next go to the upper left corner, as at C, and take the same kind of stitch. Finally proceed to the fourth corner, as at D, letting the yarn pass under the right side of the square, as at D, arrow. The needle now takes a small stitch next to point D, as shown at E, and comes under the yarn that forms the top of the square, as at F.

These four sides of the square are the foundation of the stitch. The remaining strands interweave in and

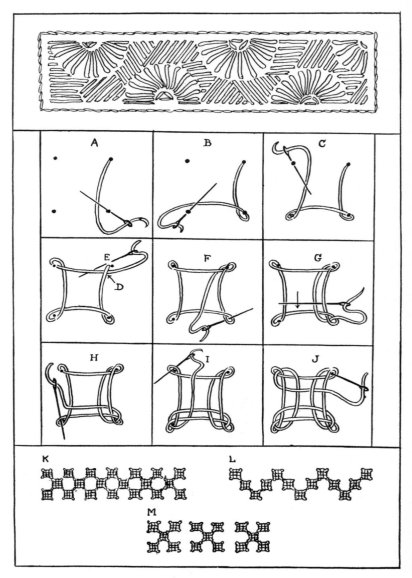

FIG. 10. SQUARE MEDALLION STITCH

out of these four sides, and are not fastened to the material underneath. The finished woven medallion, therefore, is caught down to the material only at the four corners. This makes is possible to run a ribbon through a row of the finished squares.

At *F*, in Fig. 10, the needle begins to interweave. From the top of the square the yarn goes to the opposite or bottom side and over it. Here the needle passes under the loop at the corner. Now follow the needle, as shown at *G*, from the lower right corner, passing under the first vertical strand, over the second, and over the opposite side of the square. Here the needle again goes under the corner loop, as shown at *H*. Follow the course of the yarn, as shown at *I*, under the first horizontal strand, over the second, and over the opposite side of square. Here the needle goes under the corner loop, as shown at *I*, and interweaves across to the right, as at *J*, weaving alternately under and over the strands already laid. At top right corner insert needle down into material through the loop and fasten underneath. This completes a woven medallion.

As you study the completed stitch at *J*, you will at once understand the scheme of the weaving. Every strand passes alternately under and over. Now look at *G*. Here the needle does not seem to alternate; but just imagine that there is a strand where the arrow is, as there finally will be, and that the needle is passing under this strand, as it does in the end. Then you will see that at *G*, *H*, and *I*, just as at *J*, the needle goes under the first strand, over the second, under the imaginary third one, and over the opposite side. Bear this in mind and the weaving will be simple.

The drapery border in Plate VII, on page 40, may be

PLATE VIII

A stunning scarf of brown trimmed with gold wool in
square medallion stitch (Fig. 10)

made with a row of single medallions or by using any of the plans in Fig. 10, at *K*, *L* or *M*. In Plate VIII, page 44, is shown a combination scarf and shawl made of deep brown woollen cloth, embroidered with gold wool in rows of the medallion stitch, using the design in Fig. 10, *M*. The scarf is lined with gold crêpe de Chine.

PLATE IX

A lovely scenic wall hanging embroidered in wool tones of blue, grey and tan.

Courtesy of Tina McMorran

CHAPTER VI

STITCHES SIMPLE BUT SMART

THE colour and texture of woollen yarns are so full of life and loveliness that even the simplest stitches give very smart effects. We who like to embroider, and to whom the rhythmic motion of sewing gives endless satisfaction, welcome new suggestions for combining simple and familiar stitches. Often the charm of a stitch depends upon its setting and colour. The stitches shown in Fig. 11 may be worked out in a great variety of ways.

A novel featherbone stitch worked in two colours is shown in Fig. 11, No. 1. With the darker of the two colours embroider the straight border with outline stitch. This may be made double, as shown. Down through the centre space work a simple large feather-bone stitch in the darker colour, as at *A*. Then, with the lighter colour, work a double featherbone stitch over the leaves of the first, as shown at *B* and *C*. The first of the pair of stitches is taken at the end of the leaf and over it in button-hole fashion, as at *B*; and the second stitch is taken at the base of the leaf and over it, as at *C*. Continue covering leaves at left and right. The finished stitch looks like a stem with leaves, and should measure, including border, about 1½ in. Use it at the ends of runners, around pillows or d'oyleys, or to decorate the margins of curtains.

Stitch No. 2 in Fig. 11 illustrates a border employing for its edges the couching-stitch pictured on this page

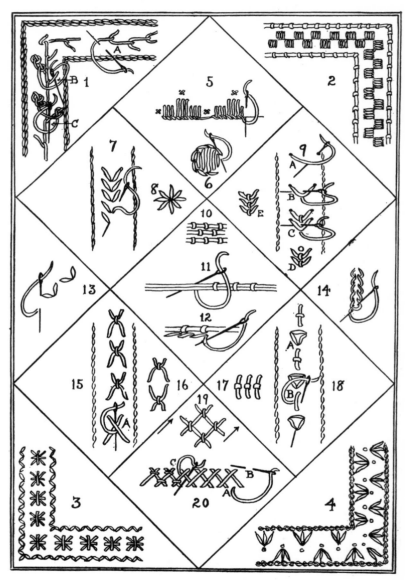

FIG. 11. STITCHES SIMPLE BUT SMART

in the space numbered 11. The intervening space is filled in with alternate squares of straight stitches, four stitches in each square. The entire border measures 1 in. to 1½ in. wide, and is best made with two or three colours.

The border at No. 3, Fig. 11, uses the stitch shown in space 13 for its two edges, and fills in the intervening space with stars of long, crossing, straight stitches. The complete border measures 1½ in. wide, and may be made all of one colour or of two colours.

The border shown in space No. 4 uses a chain-stitch for its two edges, and little pyramids composed of three stitches each for its design. These are ⅜ in. apart and ⅜ in. high, and are made preferably in a second colour. The entire border is about 1 in. wide.

The stitch in space 5 is a decorative edge. First three button-hole stitches are taken ¼ in. long, then three more are taken close to these ½ in. long, and again three more ¼ in. long. A space of about ¼ in. is left between each set of stitches. These little spaces are filled in with a cross-stitch, and a small cross-stitch is also placed at the top of each group of long stitches, as shown.

A circular motif is shown in space 6, the inside of the circle filled in with long satin-stitches, and the outer edge made with an outline stitch of the same or a contrasting colour of wool.

The border shown in space 7 consists of opposite diagonal stitches ½ in. long, meeting each other at the base. Finish one side of stitches before starting the opposite.

The rosette in space 8 is made of small, straight stitches, all having a common centre.

The stitch in space 9 is a winged stitch, very effective when grouped into butterfly or flower forms. Take a wide stitch from left to right, as in space 9, *A*, bring the needle out $\frac{1}{4}$ in. below the two upper points of stitch, then take the wool over the base of stitch, as shown at *B*, making a fastening loop. The needle point now comes out just below the beginning of first stitch at the left, ready to make a second complete stitch just below the first, as at *C*. Two stitches are effective with a centre dot, as at *D*, or several used in line, as at *E*.

A very serviceable way of making a woollen border called "couching," is shown in Fig. 11, Nos. 10, 11, and 12. Several strands of wool are laid down on the design line and fastened down with over-and-over stitches of wool in the same or a different colour, as at 11. These stitches are from $\frac{1}{4}$ in. to $\frac{1}{2}$ in. apart. At 10, several rows of couching are made parallel to fill up a solid space; and at 12 a line of couching is accented by having a line of outline embroidery close beside it. If this is of contrasting colour, it will set off the couching.

The simple border in space 13 is made of little stitches about $\frac{1}{4}$ in. long taken at an angle and facing each other.

The chain-stitch in space 14 is excellent for borders, for outlining, and for filling in rounded forms, within which it curves in spirals.

A large cross-stitch is shown in space 15, its intersection being nearer one end of the stitch than the other. A short, straight stitch holds it in place, taken as shown at *A*. Two of these stitches placed end to end, as at 16, form a figure which, if repeated, makes an effective border about 1 in. wide.

In space 17 is shown a long woollen stitch with

PLATE X

Effective borders on a homespun runner; stitches in
Chap. VI

a cross-bar at its centre. This also makes a good border.

A border of two motives is shown in space 18. The little triangles at A are placed 1 in. apart, and the $\frac{1}{2}$ in. spaces between them are filled in with the cross-bar stitches shown at 17. They are shown being made at B.

An attractive square that may be repeated in border form is shown in space 19. This is composed of four woollen stitches, each 1 in. long, and intersecting $\frac{1}{4}$ in. from the corners. This figure may be repeated from left to right, as shown here, with the points of the square at top and bottom, or the squares may be placed side by side, following the direction of the arrows.

The stitch in space 20 is a convenient border, made with a row of interlaced cross-stitches underneath and a row of fastening stitches on top. The row underneath is taken from left to right, but the needle is inserted from right to left, as shown at A and B, the threads crossing each other diagonally. The fastening stitches, worked in yarn of another colour, consist of horizontal stitches interlaced around the points of intersection of the first stitches, as shown at C.

Some of the stitches described above were used to embroider horizontal borders and zigzag ornaments on the homespun runner shown in Plate X, giving it life and interest.

CHAPTER VII

FOR richness of effect in formal rooms, the gorgeous colouring and beauty of design that characterize Jacobean embroidery are ideal. Jacobean embroidery is a term applied to the exquisite linens embroidered with wools in Britain during the Stuart period. Large rooms of oak panelling seemed to require embroideries of a substantial, dignified quality, and the rich colourings of wool gave the desired effect. Here were used against the deep rich colour of oak, impressive wall panels, decorative bedspreads, ornamental cushions, draperies, chair seats and footstools—all of elaborate design worked in subtle tones of wool. Vegetable dyes made possible clear beautiful shades that combined in producing unusual results.

The designs were mostly Oriental, brought to Britain by the East India Trading Company. All colours were employed, and a great variety of stitches—outline, chain-stitch, flat-stitch, button-holing, couching, long, and short-stitch, etc. There are many lovely designs available for this work that we can appropriate in our embroideries to-day—designs in rugs, wall panels, and elaborate costumes. When you have chosen a motif, simplify it for your purpose, and transfer it to woollen tapestry cloth, linen or monk's cloth. Choose colours that blend well together, colours of inherent richness— shades of rose and crimson, blue passing in gradations

to indigo, soft golds, russets and browns, and tones of
green and coral.

Crewel embroidery is less elaborate than Jacobean,
but equally lovely. The designs, more modern in
character, adapt bird and flower motives to centre-
pieces, table-runners, bags, book-covers, and draperies.
The patterns are applied to linens or tapestry cloth, and
worked out mostly in chain- or outline-stitches that
follow the curves, and fill in the spaces of the design
most uniformly and effectively. Every possible shade
and colour of woollen yarn result in embroideries of
satisfying depth and beauty. The wools used are made
especially for crewel embroidery and are called crewel
wools.

Some graceful forms are shown in Fig. 12 that may
be adapted to Jacobean or crewel embroidery. The
conventionalized border at *A* may be worked in chain-
or outline-stitch, and the scattered flower forms at *B*
may be used singly at the corners of pillows, table-
covers, etc., or in rows along the ends of runners and
curtain borders. They may be simply outlined with
wools, or embroidered solid in various stitches. A conventionalized urn is shown at *C*, worked out in tones of
green and coral and using chain-stitch only; and at *D*
is a splendid design for the end of a table-runner or
panel, worked out using various woolcraft stitches.
To gain a full appreciation of this very fine type of
embroidery, one should visit museums and examine the
richly embroidered tapestries of a day gone by. Here
we may gather a fund of inspiration and ideas to em-
body in the lovely objects we are seeking to create.
A most beautiful example of crewel embroidery is
shown in Plate XXI in the last chapter of this book.

FIG. 12. DESIGNS FOR CREWEL AND
JACOBEAN EMBROIDERIES

PLATE XI

Crisp gay organdie ruffles in a pink and blue bedroom are trimmed with strips of organdie stitched
with woollen yarns. Design shown in Chap. V, Fig. 10

Designed by George E. Fowler

PAINTING WITH WOOLS ON ORGANDIE

One of the sheerest of materials, organdie is strangely enough quite stunning when embellished with woollen yarns. Perhaps it is the contrast of delicate background and substantial embroidery that produces such an alluring effect. At any rate, the clear, bright colours of organdie frame floral or conventionalized designs painted in vari-coloured wools in sharp and vivid beauty.

The organdie is basted to a smooth paper to hold it fairly taut while embroidering. Any kind of woolcraft stitches may be used, the simple stitches proving very effective. Designs of the type shown in Fig. 12 for crewel embroideries are good to use. Very simple flower forms worked in a few bright colours seem to be in spirit with the delicate character of organdie.

The dainty bedroom shown in Plate XI, page 56, shows how very charming an organdie ensemble can be when accented with woollen borders. Strips of the organdie are embroidered separately with variegated shades of wool, and these strips are then applied to the top of valance and dressing-table, to the bedspread flounce, and even to the fluffy little tie-backs and dainty lampshade. The design used is shown in the top of Fig. 10, in Chapter V, on page 42. The crescents are filled in with radiating stitches, all of one colour, and in between them the irregular sections are filled in with simple over-and-over stitches, each section a different colour. Pale blue organdie with stitches mostly in tones of pink wool, or *vice versa*, is very effective. Other schemes are apricot organdie with turquoise borders, green with black and silver, yellow with orange and black, or cream with lavender or blue.

CHAPTER VIII

WOOLCRAFT APPLIQUÉ

APPLIQUÉ designs, with their myriad possible colour forms, provide a means of giving a new note to home textiles if the technique of woolcraft is used. The execution of regular appliqué is a rather irksome task, requiring the turning under of the cut edges along curves and in corners, and the difficulty of making these places neat interferes somewhat with the pleasure of the work. To provide an easier, more fascinating type of appliqué, woolcraft suggests sewing down the motives to the foundation material with a woollen stitch taken along their outlines. The stitch has body enough so that the appliqué pieces can be clipped close to its line when finished. This woollen stitch outline holds the applied pieces down firmly, besides making a most definite and attractive edge. If a striking outline is needed, the woollen stitching may be of a deep contrasting colour to the appliqué; but if one desires a softer effect, the wool may be of the same colour as the applied design. Plates XII and XIII illustrate the very striking effects of appliqué designs applied by the woolcraft method.

Outlining appliqué with wools suggests several stitches that are very appropriate. First, the woollen outline may be made with a zigzag, triangular stitch, as in Fig. 13. Second, a stitch resembling two rows of back-stitch may be used, as in Fig. 14. Again, outline or chain-stitch may be used very effectively along the edges of cut pieces of appliqué. In cutting out the parts of applied material not necessary for the design, most unique and lovely results are possible, as shown by the

PLATE XII

Boudoir bag in orchid with woolcraft edges and appliqué in wine and rose

designs in Figs. 13 and 14. The outside of the design is cut close to the woollen outline, but within the design, parts may be cut out or left, as preferred. In the curtain border in Fig. 14, *K*, the white parts are the appliqué, and the inked sections represent the material.

These might also have been cut away for a very different effect.

The following directions may be worked out by taking simple border designs or motifs from nature, and making a little appliqué pattern of them for learning the wool-craft method as applying them to a background. In wool appliqué, the piece to be applied should be of a thin material like organdie or voile, or an open-mesh material like net, theatrical gauze, loosely woven silk or wool; and the foundation material should be slightly heavier in weight like coarse linen, burlap, monk's cloth, a soft wool of loose mesh, or any material the strands of which may be pulled together a little in stitching. The design to be worked out should first be traced or outlined on the upper or appliqué material, and this then basted down along its edges to the material underneath, as in Fig. 13, *A*. A margin is always left outside of the traced design as shown.

The woollen stitching is now applied along the outline, as shown in Fig. 13, *B*. This is described in detail below. Finally, the upper material is cut off up to the woollen stitching along its edge, as shown in Fig. 13, *C*, and the coloured appliqué, *D*, is left, fastened down to the foundation material. Connections may be made between motifs by embroidering stems, lines, etc., with the stitch alone, and parts of the appliqué may be cut out within the outer border, leaving lovely openwork effects.

BORDER STITCH IN FIG. 13. This triangular stitch takes up about ¼ in. space along the edge of the appliqué. The outer line of the traced design will be the outside edge of the stitches when finished. The dots in the drawings of Fig. 13 show the points the needle enters,

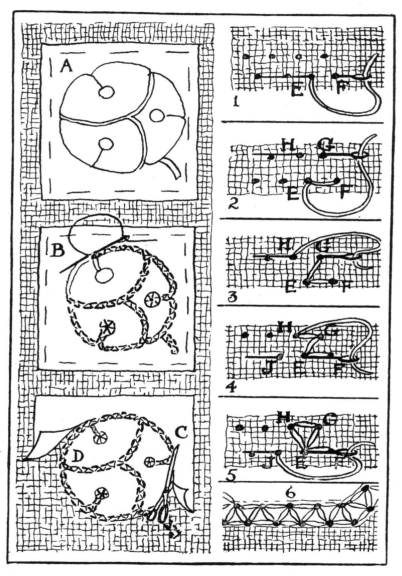

FIG. 13. TRIANGULAR EDGE FOR WOOLCRAFT APPLIQUÉ

but the stitch is worked without any guide points, as one can measure with the eye successive distances of $\frac{1}{4}$ in. The stitching goes from right to left.

Fig. 13, space 1. The needle comes out at E, $\frac{1}{4}$ in. from start at right, goes in at F, $\frac{1}{4}$ in. to the right, and comes out at E again.

Space 2. The needle has taken first stitch, EF, and now goes in at G, midway between E and F, on row above, $\frac{1}{4}$ in. away. The needle, entering at G, comes out at H, $\frac{1}{4}$ in. to its left.

Space 3. The needle has made stitch EF and stitch EG, and now goes in at G and out at H a second time.

Space 4. The needle has completed stitches EF, EG, and GH, and now goes back to E in lower row, where it starts $\frac{1}{4}$ in. to left again, coming out at J.

Space 5. Stitches EF, EG, GH, and HE are now complete, and the needle is proceeding with a new stitch to the left, as was begun in space 1, from F to E. Continue repeating the above.

Space 6. The appearance of the finished stitch is that of successive triangles pulled tightly together. This is the stitch used in the boudoir bag of Plate XII.

BORDER STITCH IN FIG. 14. Fig. 14 shows another stitch equally effective, but taken from left to right, contrary to the above stitch.

Fig. 14, space 1. The stitching travels along two horizontal lines like that in Fig. 13, and these are about $\frac{1}{4}$ in. apart. The needle comes out at A, goes in at B, $\frac{1}{4}$ in. to the right, and out at C, midway between A and B and $\frac{1}{4}$ in. above them.

Space 2. The needle comes out at C and goes in at D, $\frac{1}{4}$ in. to the right, and out at B on lower line.

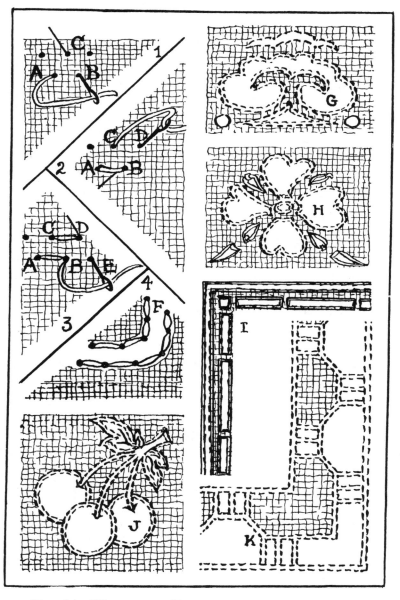

FIG. 14. WOOLCRAFT EDGE OF PARALLEL STITCHES

Space 3. The needle has made stitches AB and CD and is now ready to start to the right as in space 1, entering at E, which corresponds to B.

Space 4. The stitch is here shown complete. Underneath these two simple lines of stitching there is a meshwork of the strands as they pass underneath in taking the steps, and it is this that holds the appliqué so firmly at its edges. The porch set in Plate XIII may be decorated with this stitch or the one in Fig. 13.

At Fig. 14, G, H, I, and J are shown types of woolcraft appliqué designs.

Both of the above stitches, Figs. 13 and 14, may be used decoratively without any appliqué, and in Fig. 15 is shown a third stitch that makes most attractive geometrical designs with wool on cloth showing a cross-weave similar to linen-weave.

DESIGN STITCH IN FIG. 15. This stitch is similar to Italian hemstitching, and makes pleasing openwork design lines on a mesh material. It is useful for doilies, curtains, chair-backs, mats, and many straight line borders. The value of this stitch is that it will travel along a diagonal line, and regular Italian hemstitching, described in the next chapter, may accompany it to travel along the horizontal and vertical lines of a design.

Fig. 15, space 1. The needle enters at A, goes to B, $\frac{1}{4}$ in. above, and comes out at A again.

Space 2. The needle enters at B again and comes out at C, $\frac{1}{4}$ in. to the left.

Space 3. From C, the needle is again inserted at B and comes out at C.

Space 4. From C, the needle goes to step D, $\frac{1}{4}$ in. above C, and comes out at C again. The needle is now

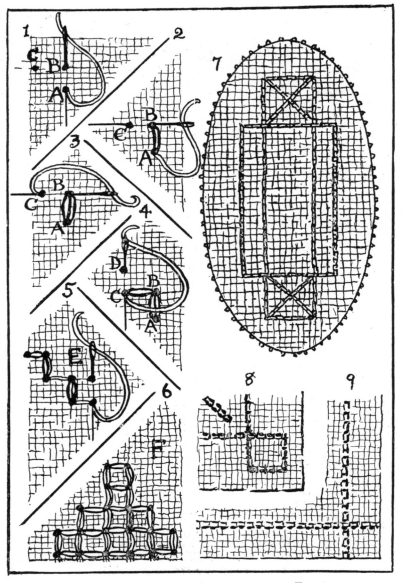

FIG. 15. STITCH FOR OPENWORK ON DOILIES
AND CURTAINS

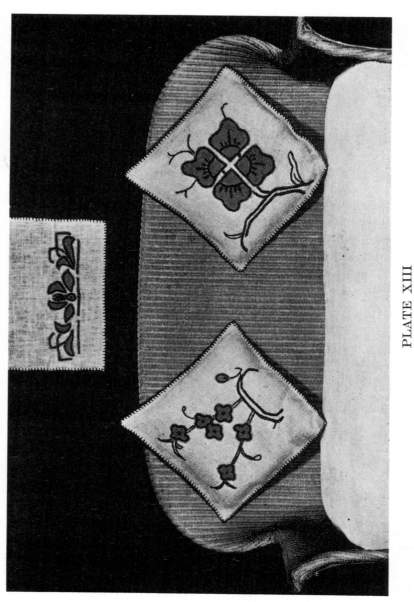

PLATE XIII

Bright red appliqué motifs stitched to linen backgrounds with black wool; stitches in
Fig. 13, Chap. VIII

in the position shown in space 1, from *B* to *A*, and repeats the stitches just described.

Space 5. When the first diagonal row is finished, start another as shown at *E*.

Space 6. This stitch makes a kind of ladder along homespun or mesh cloth. Spaces may be filled in with it as shown at *F*, so that it is convenient to use for making solid designs.

Space 7. A square, round or oval doily may have as its sole trimming this delightful mesh embroidery with wools. The diagonal lines are worked as just described. The straight lines are worked with the corresponding straight mesh-stitch known as Italian hemstitch and described in Chapter IX, Fig. 16.

Space 8. The corners of square doilies, and the borders and corners of draperies and couch covers of mesh materials, may be trimmed very easily with lines of mesh hemstitching, as shown.

Space 9. A simple border is shown here, made of Italian hemstitching 2 in. or 3 in. from the edge of the material.

The stitches described above, in dark-coloured wools against bright backgrounds make very effective decorative accessories. The cushions and runner in Plate XIII were very quickly embroidered with woolcraft appliqué stitches in black on red designs—all against a natural background.

CHAPTER IX

CROSS-STITCH AND ASSISI WORK WITH WOOLS

EVERYONE loves to embroider cross-stitch patterns, and in wools they are charmingly effective on backgrounds of coarse linen, burlap, monk's cloth or any mesh material. The opposite of cross-stitch, Assisi work, in which the design is left unembroidered and the entire background filled in with cross-stitch, is equally attractive. Just one colour is used for the background, accenting the light-coloured design space left on the material. Porch sets made up in a coarse mesh with either of these stitches for ornament have a smart appearance. The best colours to use against a cream or neutral background are bright red, blue, brown, green and purple. Touches of black always add character. The frontispiece shows cross-stitch designs on monk's cloth cushions, with borders in cross-stitch to match.

PATTERNS TO USE. Any pattern worked out on check paper is adaptable. Animal patterns are interesting and quaint. Choose those whose members are well outlined, such as the duck with his long neck, the camel with his hump, the elephant with his trunk, or the stag with his graceful antlers. Flowers are equally interesting and are often conventionalized to use between animal designs. To change any drawing into a cross-stitch or Assisi pattern, trace it on checked paper, then with a pencil, outline the checks that are closest to the lines of the drawing. Emphasize any characteristic parts by making them a trifle large. Paint in the design or its background with ink to get its effect.

PREPARING THE MATERIAL. Finishing the edge of the material before embroidering prevents its fraying and enables one to place the design more accurately with reference to the edge. Any of the woollen edges in Chapter IV may be used, and the cross-stitch border

Courtesy Ramapo Arts and Crafts Centre
PLATE XIV
Designs in cross-stitch on burlap market bags

in Chapter IV, Fig. 7, is especially suitable. For Assisi patterns, Italian hemstitch is used a great deal, as Assisi work was first done by Italian women many hundreds of years ago.

ITALIAN HEMSTITCH. All material for hemming should be cut along the straight line made by a drawn thread. Overcast the cut edge with thread and needle to prevent fraying. Allow ⅜ in. to ¾ in. distance from the edge for the final hem. At the inner edge of this margin draw two threads. Now skip three, four, or five threads toward inside of cloth and draw two more threads. There are now two lines of drawn threads open for the Italian hemstitch, as shown in Fig. 16, upper diagram, space 1, arrows. The space in between, i.e. the number of threads skipped, determines the width of the hemstitching.

To begin the stitch, fasten a thread to the corner and bring it out four or more threads to the left, as in Fig. 16, *A*. Any number of threads may be taken for the group between *A* and *B*, but the same number must be taken at each stitch. Back-stitch to the starting point, *B*, and insert needle diagonally under the material, bringing it out at *C*, opposite *A*, on the other row of pulled threads. Now back-stitch the same number of threads to the right, insert needle at *D*, and bring it out again at *C*. Now carry needle to opposite point, *A*, insert, and take up a group to the left, bringing needle out at *E*, as shown in the third drawing. This finishes one complete stitch. From point *E* proceed as from point *A*, and continue thus all around edge of material. The finished hemstitching is shown at *F*. The woollen yarn should be pulled rather tight in stitching to give the best effect. When the stitching is finished, turn under the hem at the outer edge, and hem with needle and thread close up to the hemstitching. If one of the drawn threads is used, this hemming will not show.

OUTLINING THE PATTERN FOR ASSISI WORK. To get the design on the cloth is the next problem. You do this by counting off a certain number of mesh threads for each little square given in the pattern. The number you decide upon is the same as the number of threads

Courtesy Italian Needlework Guild, New York City

PLATE XV

Elephant design in white cross-stitch outlined in
black on a pink linen laundry bag

you will put into each cross-stitch. In coarse material, take up three or four threads to a stitch; in finer material, six or more. This little group of threads taken up for a single stitch, uses up a square on the cloth corresponding to a like square on the pattern.

In Assisi work the outline of the design as well as its background is stitched in with wools, using a running-stitch, as shown in Fig. 16, *G*. Begin at a corner of the design and run the needle under the number of threads chosen for a square, and then over the same number, in and out, as shown. When the needle has gone all around the design, retrace its course, and go over where before you stitched under the cloth, etc., as shown at Fig. 16, *H*, until there is a continuous outline as shown at *I*. In the animal designs shown in this chapter the figures are outlined in this way. At the drawing in Fig. 16, *O*, these outline stitches are clearly seen at the arrow.

CROSS-STITCHING THE BACKGROUND. Each check or square in the patterns shown represents the space allowed for a cross-stitch, and each cross-stitch on the pattern is transferred to the cloth by counting off threads, as just described. Each cross-stitch also takes up the same number of threads as that allowed for an outline-stitch. Each cross-stitch of the filling in is taken by counting this same number of threads to the left of the last stitch and the same number of threads above it, as shown by the needle at *O*. Stitch from right to left on a horizontal line, as at *J*, and at the end of a row return to the right, completing each cross-stitch, as shown at *K*. As each row is completed, take the next horizontal row above. The finished background is shown at *M*. An extra line of cross-stitching at top and

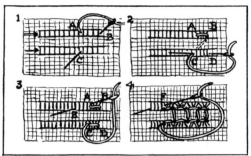

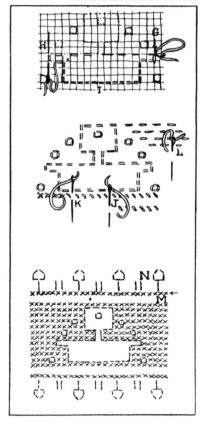

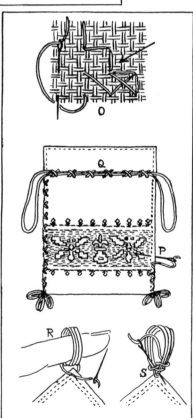

FIG. 16. ITALIAN HEMSTITCH AND ASSISI WORK

bottom is effective, with a blank row left between it
and the main background, as at *M*, arrow.

PLATE XVI
Panel design planned for a cross-stitch background
Designed by Frank B. Couch

BORDER STITCHES. Sometimes a delicate border
design is added, as shown in Fig. 16, *N*. This should be
in character with the rest of the design, and is worked
in the same running-stitch used to outline the design,

running in spaced stitches first, then filling up the spaces on the return trip. Back-stitch may also be used.

To-day Assisi backgrounds are sometimes filled in with other stitches quicker than cross-stitch in their execution. One of these is the seed-stitch, a running-stitch going in and out of the groups of threads as shown in Fig. 16, *L*. Woollen yarns are especially adaptable to the seed-stitch, filling in the spaces rapidly. A space is left between the design outline and the background made with the seed-stitch.

THING TO MAKE. Bags, runners, pin-cushions, sofa cushions, curtains, scarves and wall panels—all lend themselves readily to varieties of cross-stitch. In drawing two hemstitched edges together, do so by using the cross-stitch edge as shown in Fig. 16, *P*. Edges of bags and cushions are attractive finished in this way. To make a path for the draw cord, execute a line of cross-stitches on either side of a bag, as shown at *Q*.

Little tasselled loops are often added to this work at the corners. They are made as shown at *R* and *S*. Hold the edge of material up, catch the wool through the hemstitch, and wrap the wool around the left forefinger several times.   Bring the wool back to starting point at the edge or corner, and slip the finger out, still holding the loops together between left thumb and forefinger. With wool and needle in the right hand, weave in and out of the two groups of wool several times, close to the edge, as shown at *S*, finally fastening the wool back through the weaving, or continuing in another loop. Rows of loops are put along the edges of runners, curtains or scarves. Several loops are bunched together at the corners of cushions or bags.

The animal patterns shown in Plates XVI and XVII,

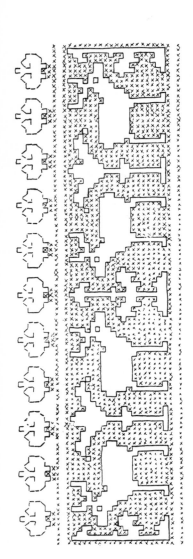

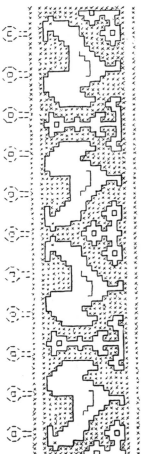

PLATE XVII

Animal patterns charming for use in children's rooms

Designed by Frank B. Couch

make good ends for runners or wall panels in a child's room. The entire pattern may be used, or any motif used separately. For the elephant pattern, use a white or cream material, and work the background in deep blue, red, brown or black. For the stag pattern, tan linen cross-stitched with red would be nice, or in place of red, dark brown or green. For the cock pattern, use cream, yellow or orange linen with design or background in red, green or brown. Each pattern may be reversed to make into cross-stitch instead of Assisi work.

CHAPTER X

NET-WEAVING is made easy by the very nature of the materials used in working. One starts with a piece of coarse, substantial net or linen, and a handful of wool. All one needs to know is a stitch or two with which to fill the squares, and with these a variety of designs can be developed. There are so many ways of filling in the squares of net, that only a few can be given here; but one can combine these in many ways, and even invent new stitches. The patterns are easy to follow, as they are given on checked paper, and any filet pattern may be used. Almost any kind of open net can be worked up into attractive articles. You will find on sale coarse mesh nets, lace nets, and various fancy varieties. There is also a strong fibrous net made for the purposes of weaving durable and beautiful objects, such as envelope purses, chair seats, stool covers, pillow tops, table-mats, rugs, bags, luncheon sets, and bedspreads. In Plate XVIII, page 79, the window grouping of draperies, valance and table-cover embroidered with wools on net is a fine example of the simplicity and dignity achieved by the use of net-weaving technique.

THE SIMPLEST STITCH. The simplest stitch to use on the net is a straight over-and-over stitch, shown in Fig. 17, *A* to *H*. The wool enters a square of the net from above, as shown at *A*, passes under the two squares just below the entering square, and comes out at *B*. This is the start. Now comes the first regular stitch. The

needle goes over two squares directly over *B*, entering
the starting square, as shown at *C*, making the first
vertical stitch. Now the needle comes out one square

PLATE XVIII
A living-room ensemble with floral design in net
weaving
Designed by George E. Fowler

to the left of the base of the first stitch, i.e. at *D*. The
next stitch takes in the two squares directly above *D*,
entering at *E*, and comes out at *F*, the next square to
the left of *D*. The end, *G*, is concealed by the stitches.
Each stitch covers two vertical squares, and comes out

just one square to the left of base of last stitch ready
to start a new one.

The base of the next row of stitches is the same row
of squares as formed the top of the first row, as shown
at H, and no thread of the material is left between rows.
This same over-and-over stitching may be taken horizontally as well as vertically.

The edges of doilies and bags are treated as shown
in Fig. 17, J. Two or three squares are folded over,
then the stitches are taken over the double net, preferably going over the edges, as shown at K. Button-
holing is also effective, as at L.

A PATTERN OF STEPS. For diagonal effects, stitch in
a pattern of steps, as shown in Fig. 17, M to O. The stitch
is started as described above, and for each stitch the
needle covers two complete vertical squares; but the
needle enters one square higher at each stitch to the
left, as shown at N, and omits one square at the base of
the stitch in starting. For the next row above, the
base of each stitch is in the same square as was entered
for the top of the stitch beneath. For the edge of this
stitch, a narrow row of plain over-and-over stitches
is used, as shown at O, the stitches in the row below
being shortened to make a straight edge next to row O.

LONG AND SHORT STITCH. In this stitch the long and
short stitches of adjacent rows alternate and fit into
each other as in Fig. 17, P. The needle takes up three
complete vertical squares for the first stitch, being
inserted into the fourth square above the starting
square. For the second stitch, the needle drops a
square at both top and bottom, stitching around one
complete square only, as shown at Q, where the needle,
having taken a short stitch, comes out one square below

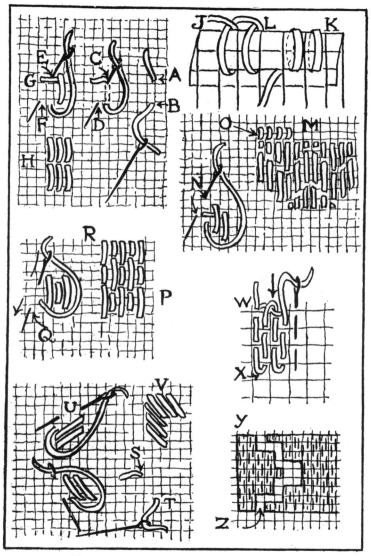

FIG. 17. NET WEAVING DIAGRAMS

its starting point and to the left. From this point the needle takes up three complete vertical squares again, entering the fourth, as shown by the arrow above Q. For the row of stitches above this one, the long stitches come above the short stitches, and *vice versa*. For an edge where this stitch is used, bring the stitches up to a straight line, as shown at R.

DIAGONAL STITCH. This is a regular over-and-over stitch, but worked on a diagonal line. Enter the needle as in Fig. 17, S, then bring it out two squares to the right and two squares downward as at T. This establishes the diagonal, and the first stitch is taken entering at S. Bring needle out one square to the left of T for next stitch, and insert it one square to the left of S. The same stitch may be used horizontally, as at ST, or vertically, as at U. A corner is shown at V. By combining this diagonal stitch with straight stitches, contrast of texture is obtained, and the net weaving takes on a modern aspect, in which masses of stitches going in one direction are accented by adjacent stitches going in another direction.

FILET WEAVING-STITCH. Filet weaving-stitch is the same as that used for making real filet lace when filling in the squares. The yarn moves in and out, passing back and forth twice in each line of squares, as in Fig. 17, W. The stitch is the same on both sides and, therefore, splendid for making curtain ornaments, runners, etc. The wool enters the net at square W, and goes in and out of the squares as far as this portion of the design indicates, to X. Here it turns, goes around a thread, and then travels back through the same squares, but this time under where before it went over, and over where before it went under, as shown. At the end of this row of squares it enters the next row, as at arrow. Any ends left by a change of colour or by starting are concealed in the weaving.

Filet weaving may be continued for any number of squares. A section of a pattern is shown in Fig. 17, *Y*. The best net to use has from six to ten meshes in an inch. In filet weaving the background may be filled in, using a colour to set off the design, or it may be left unwoven, a line of empty squares being shown at *Z*. The latter is the prettier method for fine effects, resembling lace, and permitting of being lined, with colourful silk showing through.

UNDERARM PURSES. Underarm purses may be made of net, linen or homespun, embroidered with net-weaving stitches. A piece of net 48 in. wide will make three purses, each purse measuring 12 in. by 16 in. unfolded. When folded, each purse measures about 5 in. by 10 in. The three sections are labelled *A*, *B*, and *C*, in Fig. 18. *A* is the front and may be cut in any shape, *B* is the back, and *C* the centre when folded in and sewed to the back, *B*. Both *A* and *C* are ¼ in. to ½ in. less than *B* in width.

Begin the purse by putting the design on the front, *A*. The easiest method is to embroider the design first, then its background. After finishing flap, *A*, embroider back, *B*, with a simple design or just a border ornament, and finally fill in section *C* with plain in-and-out weaving, or leave it plain if the material used is homespun. To make the purse easier to fold, one or two threads of the net may be overcast across the folding line as shown in Fig. 18, *D*. Next, stitch the border around flap *A*, from *E* to *F*, as shown at *J*, and also stitch border at the back edge, *GH*. The rest of the edge at

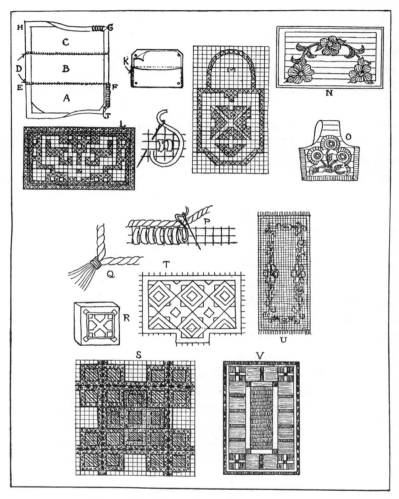

FIG. 18. NET WEAVING DESIGNS

the sides is left unfinished for the present. Cover the entire surface of the embroidered purse with a damp cloth and press flat. Sew a flat lining of silk, turned under at its edges, to the inside of the flat purse. This lining should come up to the line of the sewn border, J. Now fold the purse over with the edges of B and C together, and stitch their sides together with over-and-over stitches, as shown at K.

A conventionalized design for a bag is shown in Fig. 18, L. This design may also be used for a pointed front by leaving off the two lower corners. At M is shown a design for a market bag. The back and front are stitched separately, each piece is then cut up to the line of the design, and the two pieces are then sewed together at their edges. A piece of embroidered net may be used for the handle, or a strip of net may be rolled into tube-form, and stitched into a rope-like affair by means of button-hole stitches.

At N a different type of design is shown. Here the forms are embroidered with wool and the background filled in with plain net-weaving stitches. At O an arm-bag is made of a piece of net folded over double from the base, cut to shape, and embroidered. The background stitches are plain.

RUNNERS, RUGS AND CUSHIONS. All kinds of household articles are easy to make up with net. Choose an appropriate pattern, measure off the net to be used, embroider design, and press under a damp cloth. Edges may be finished as described above, or a twisted rope, made of two or three strands of wool may be sewn to the edge as shown in Fig. 18, P. The rope may be bound into a tassel at the corners, as shown at Q.

Good designs for pillows and mats are shown at R and

PLATE XIX

Drawn-work darned in wools on a burlap foundation

S, and at *T* is shown a pattern for a purse, bag or chair-back. *U* is a filet pattern to be worked on fine net, and *V* is a rug or tile design to be embroidered with wools on burlap.

The market bag in Plate XIX, page 86, combines use with beauty in being made of strong burlap and ornamented with interwoven stitches in bright wools. The threads of the cloth are drawn for a space of two or three inches, and the interweaving worked over the groups of the warp threads left standing. The method is clearly visible. The colours used were bright orange, yellow and green, with black outlines and French dots above and below. This kind of woollen embroidery is called Swedish weaving, and there are many ways of grouping the threads to be woven, and of making borders of several rows of the openwork.

CHAPTER XI

DARNING on theatrical gauze or fine nets, such as scrim or any curtain net material, has the simplicity of all truly artistic things, for the outlines of the work are delicately suggestive, and the art lies in subtle colour combinations rather than in a difficult manner of working. Interesting motifs are applied to the gauze with a transfer pattern, or suggested with chalk outlines, and the spaces are then filled in with parallel lines of in-and-out darning. A simple stitch of this kind offers a wide range of expression to the creative worker, especially to the person who appreciates the lovely gradations of colour tones in wool. It is really like painting with wools—filling in the design with the soft delicate fibres so beautifully dyed.

Regulation theatrical gauze, or a similar material, is used for the darning foundation. If a transfer pattern is available, apply directly to the gauze. Another reliable method of making the design visible is to draw the design on smooth white drawing paper, with strong outlines. The gauze or net is then laid over the design and basted down, as shown in Fig. 19, *A*. The net is transparent and the pattern shows through, as at *B*. The darning may be done in and out of the net without going through to the paper underneath. The stitches are taken as shown in Fig. 19, *C*, over two threads and under two threads alternately. Fairly fine wool is used. In doing a border design like that at *D*, only a part of

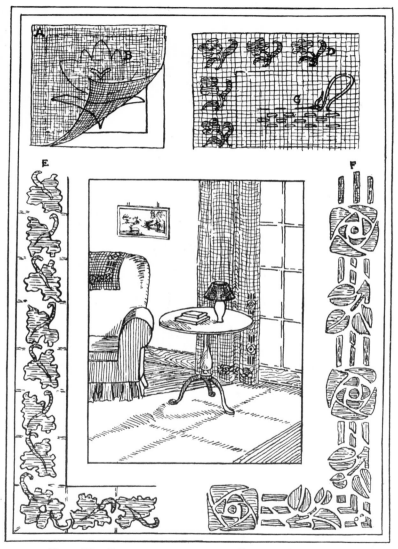

FIG. 19. ILLUSTRATIONS FOR GAUZE DARNING

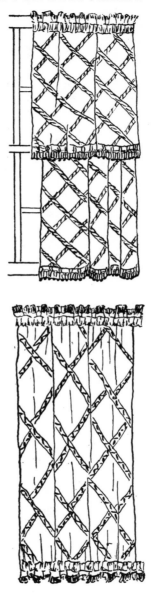

FIG. 20. SHEER CURTAINS WITH DIAMOND DESIGN

the design need be put on the paper, and after stitching over it once it may be moved along and used again and again.

Designs may be darned on small pieces of theatrical gauze, and these may be appliquéd to other materials— to the front of a bag, to the corners of a bridge cover, or to ends of scarves. A long strip may be darned in bright wools and used to trim the bedroom, in the same way that organdie strips were used in Chapter VII. Bags may be made of theatrical gauze with bright linings underneath. Silk or sateen linings show through the gauze with lustre, and give it body and character. A living-room ensemble may be toned to a richer harmony if the colours of the rug are caught up and echoed in the woollen darning of theatrical gauze draperies. In the studio or craft room the soft tone and texture of gauze and wool accessories have a character quite in keeping with the atmosphere of creative art. The delicate tones of gauze may become backgrounds for garden-like arrays of gay flowers, leaves, birds, and insects.

The border design in Fig. 19, *E*, is of indefinite leaf forms. The more conventionalized design at *F* is used in the living-room shown, as a border for the hangings and chair-back, while a lampshade of gauze lined with silk has a flower motif done in wools. In Fig. 20 are suggestions for hall or bathroom curtains of gauze or net, crossed with diagonal lines of woollen stitching, either in-and-out darning or outline stitching.

CHAPTER XII

ONE of the most necessary and convenient articles for the tourist is a soft, cushiony mat to provide comfort when travel becomes a bit tiresome. The same mat may be used when picnicking *en route* to protect one's dress when a rock or grassy knoll is the only seat available. The grass mat is a light, convenient thing to carry, and is decorated very simply with gay woollen colours. At home the same mat is convenient for the summer porch, for often the guests outnumber the seating capacity; and a mat is so readily adjusted to any nook or corner that many people prefer it to a chair.

These mats are made with two pieces of grass matting, painted, or embroidered with wool. The pieces are sewn together, then stuffed, and the result is a light, durable mat that can be tucked under the arm and carried anywhere. The mats may be round, square or oblong. The best material to use is fibre matting or Japanese matting, available in department stores; and the plain matting called teabale, that comes wrapped around your groceryman's chests of tea, is very good to use, and as it is generally discarded may be had for the asking. One square yard of matting will make two mats 18 in. square or two round ones 18 in. in diameter.

Two pieces of matting are needed for each mat. To get a large circle trace around a large, round utensil; to get a perfect square use square and ruler. Cut the pieces the actual size the mat is to be when finished, from 15 in. to 20 in. across. To keep the pieces from fraying, stitch around the edge with a sewing machine.

FIG. 21. GIRL MAKING PORCH MAT

The design is embroidered with wools. The needle of wool is caught through straws of the matting as at *A*, and sometimes a second thread is twisted around the first as at *B*. Centres are put on as at *C*, solid stitching as at *D*. If one paints the design first, the objects may be outlined with bright coloured wools after the paint dries

Over this sew a band of fancy braid or bright coloured cotton tape to match the design on the mat. This forms a decorative edge, as shown in the drawing of Fig. 21 at the arrow.

A design may be applied to each piece of matting, or

just the top piece may be decorated. Draw the design on heavy drawing paper or strong brown wrapping paper; then cut out the forms like a stencil. Lay this paper on the matting and draw through the holes with a soft pencil or crayon. Transfer designs may be used if available. Designs may also be applied freehand with chalk. This rubs off entirely with a cloth, so that one may improve the design in applying. The final design is outlined with pale ink and the chalk wiped off.

The pieces of matting for square mats may be turned under at the edges instead of being bound with tape. To do this, cut the two pieces, allowing 2 in. extra on all sides for turning under. Cut away a little of the turn-under at the corners to prevent bulkiness. Baste down with strong thread or string. The edges of the two pieces are sewn together with wools, as shown in Fig. 22, A, described below.

There are several ways to develop the design. It may be outlined with woollen stitches and some parts filled in while others are left open. Another way is to paint the design on the matting with oil colours, let dry, and then outline it with bright colours of wool. This makes a very pretty mat. The stitch used for outlining the design is shown in Fig. 21 at A, just a simple running stitch. The needle is slipped under strands of the matting at intervals of $\frac{1}{2}$ in. to 1 in. A second strand may be twisted around the first, giving it a heavy rope effect, as shown at B. A back-stitch is also effective for outlining, or, if the matting is pliable, an outline-stitch. The centres of flowers may be embroidered as shown at C, and the parts to be made solid are filled in with plain over-and-over stitches, as shown at D. Many other stitches are adaptable.

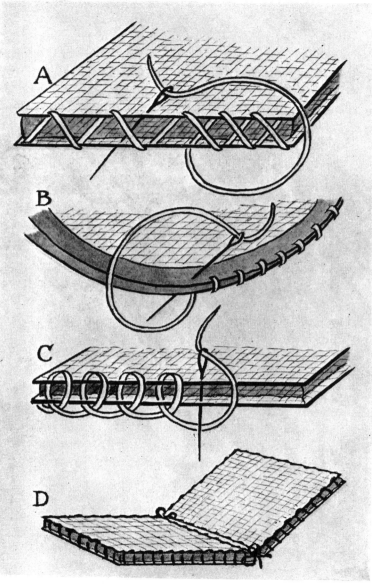

FIG. 22. DIAGRAMS FOR MAKING MATS

Before sewing the mats together, make the cushion. To do this, cut two pieces of unbleached muslin $\frac{1}{2}$ in. larger than the mat all around. Sew these together and stuff. Tack through the pad at intervals to keep the stuffing distributed evenly. The pad should be 2 in. or 3 in. thick when finished, and this gradually mats down to less than 2 in.

You are now ready to sew the two pieces of matting together. Three methods are shown in Fig. 22. If the edges have been turned under, they may be held together by woollen stitching, as shown in Fig. 22, A. One first stitches around the mat edges with straight, diagonal stitches; then the mat is turned over, and one proceeds in the opposite direction, making a final cross-stitched edge.

If the two pieces of matting have been edged with braid, they are drawn togther at their edges with a strong piece of yarn, as at B, and, just before closing, the pad is inserted.

At C in Fig. 22, a button-hole edge is used. Turn the mat upside down so that the edge of the button-holing will be on the upper side of mat when finished. The upper edge is shown underneath in the drawing at C. The charm of this edge and also of that at A is that the inner pad shows through the woollen stitching; and if this is covered with a bright cloth in contrast to the woollen edge, the effect is unique.

Two finished mats, if fastened together along one side, make a jolly little protective seat to use in a car, one mat for the back rest, and the other to sit upon, as shown in Fig. 22, D. Such an arrangement can be made very decorative as a bright spot of colour in the car, besides providing comfort to the occupants.

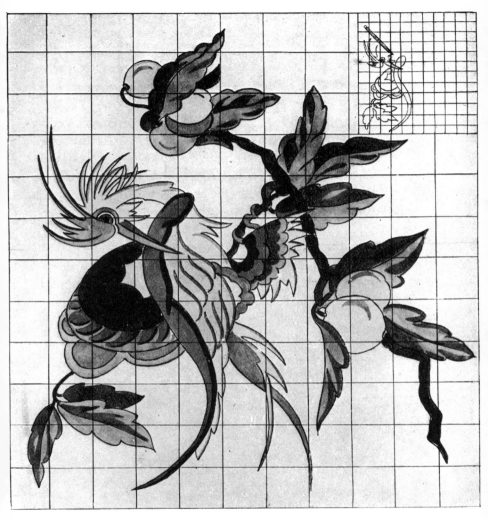

PLATE XX

Colourful bird design, drawn to scale, described on page 98.

Designed by Alexandra Croasdaile

COLOURFUL FLOWER AND BIRD DESIGNS.

This is the type design welcomed for colourful porch mats. The bird is orange and yellow with back of blue and head feathers of green; the flowers are in deep blues, greens, flame, and yellow; the fruits are orange and yellow; and the leaves, green.

The design is shown in Plate XX. To enlarge, draw off the same number of squares on a piece of drawing paper, making them as large as is necessary. Then find where the design lines cross the lines of the squares, mark these points on the larger drawing, and fill in each square with the corresponding forms in the squares of Plate XX. The method is shown in the upper right corner of Plate XX. Any of the designs given in this book may be enlarged by covering them with squares, and duplicating the contents of each square in the corresponding squares of a larger drawing.

CHAPTER XIII

WOOLCRAFT ON FELT AND OILCLOTH

FELT and oilcloth, because of their firm, substantial texture, make home accessories that are particularly smart when embroidered in colours of woollen yarn. So much can be done with a little spare time and the use of these very practical mediums for embroidery or appliqué. The highly reflective surface of oilcloth, and the heavy mat-like quality of felt, both coming in a wide range of colour, form excellent backgrounds for woollen designs in soft, subtle shades.

WOOLCRAFT ON OILCLOTH. Oilcloth trimmed with wool makes a great variety of useful household things, like cushions, book-covers, basket-covers, dust-bags, shoe-bags, doilies, screens, and floor mats. With its highly glazed surface reflecting light and colour, it is especially practical in the nursery and the kitchen, where cheer and cleanliness are essential. Black is a very popular colour, and makes a strong background for wools of any tone.

Oilcloth is used in the kitchen or nursery in place of cloth draperies, as shown in Fig. 23, *A*. The curtains are of red oilcloth embroidered with black wools, or black trimmed with corn colour, blue or green. There are so many shades of oilcloth that just the right colour for any room may be chosen. The valance of the curtains is fastened down to the side drapes with a vertical row of cross-stitching. All the edges of the curtain and tie-backs are finished with the cross-stitch edge shown in Chapter IV, Fig. 7.

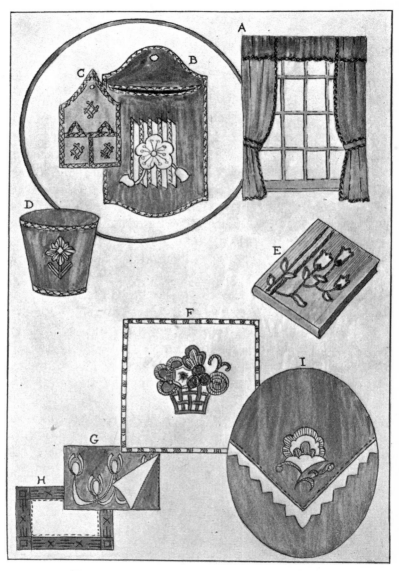

FIG. 23. WOOL ON FELT AND OILCLOTH

The objects in the circle may match the curtains. The useful laundry bag at *B* is made of two pieces of oilcloth held together at the edges with cross-stitching, and a cut opening near the top also has the cross-stitched edge. Before joining the back and front of the bag, embroider a simple design on the latter. This may be in cross-stitch or in oilcloth appliqué. The design shown has a bright oilcloth flower appliquéd at the centre, and vertical bars of cross-stitching in the background.

The hanging pocket at *C* is made like the bag, with two cut pieces of oilcloth stitched together with a woollen edging.

A practical idea for a waste basket is shown at *D*. It is made of black oilcloth with a bright orange appliquéd flower of oilcloth attached to its background with wool. To make the basket, take a piece of oilcloth large enough to encircle a tin scrap basket, sew on the oilcloth appliqué with wool button-holing, and then paste the oilcloth down on the tin, turning over its edges at top and bottom. You may also paste the oilcloth to a cardboard cylinder that is slipped over the basket as a decorative cover.

Pillows of oilcloth will stand much knocking about. Apply oilcloth appliqué designs to them, or simply embroider sprays of woollen flowers at the centre or in one corner. Lastly, there is the very successful use of oilcloth as a telephone-book cover, as shown in Fig. 23, *E*. A piece of oilcloth is decorated with outline or chain stitches in wool, and is then pasted down over a cardboard cover that fits the 'phone book. A 'phone screen may be made to match the cover. Purchase a small cardboard screen or a wire screen frame, stretch the oilcloth over this, and stitch around the edges with woolcraft stitches.

WOOLCRAFT ON FELT. We have used all kinds of backgrounds for woollen stitches—nets, linens, sheer fabrics like organdie, stiff surfaces like matting, soft silks of loose texture, and the glossy sheen of oilcloth. But none of these can surpass felt in its adaptability to woollen yarn. Felt and worsted seem to cling together, perhaps because both are made in different ways from the sheep's fibre, the felt made of matted wool and the worsted yarn of spun wool. At any rate, woollen designs on soft felt backgrounds, with an infinite variety of colour combinations to choose from, furnish some of our softest and loveliest home ornaments.

Felt appliqué, too, makes many gratifying accessories. The design is first traced or drawn with crayon on the felt foundation. The various parts of the design are then cut out of various coloured felts and laid down flat on the felt background, each in its place. The edges are now fastened down with button-holing, long and short stitches, chain-stitch or outline stitch. The appliquéd design may be further decorated with woollen embroidery.

Gay pillows of felt, trimmed with appliqué or any of the woolcraft stitches described in foregoing chapters, brighten up the window seat or the corners of the day-bed. The edges may be finished with any of the stitches in Chapter IV or Chapter VI. The pillow in Fig. 23, *F*, is of dark brown felt with an appliquéd basket design of tan, orange, yellow, and a touch of red.

An under-arm purse of deep purple felt, embroidered with solid forms in peach and orchid, is shown at *G*. The sides are bound together with woollen stitches to match the felt. The lining is peach.

At *H* we have an attractive border design that may

be applied to the edges of mats, pillows or table-runners. The stitches are long, straight ones, the parallel lines of one colour, and the crosses of a contrasting colour.

The bridge cover at *I* is of black felt with a bright blue felt border, cut into points at the edge and attached to the black felt with a blue running stitch. The appliquéd flower has a blue cup-like base, and a flower of orange and blue felt fastened down with orange and blue wool. The leaves are embroidered with green. Black felt combines well with almost any colour to make a table-cover similar to this. Good combinations are black and coral, black and green, black and pale purple, black and orange, and black and red.

In the following chapter you will find a list of splendid colour combinations to use in doing woolcraft embroidery, and also a list of the fabrics most suitable for the stitches described in this book.

CHAPTER XIV

WOOLCRAFT BACKGROUNDS AND COLOUR SCHEMES

CERTAIN materials, because of their weave and texture, are more adaptable than others to woolcraft stitchery. Soft woollen fabrics, meshes or nets, loosely woven silks or mercerized cloths, cotton crêpes, and coarse linens seem to make the most successful backgrounds. Different materials require different thicknesses of wool. To find the right size strand to use on a fabric, experiment with the odds and ends of wools in your basket, and purchase the chosen colours in the size found to be correct. In general, the following combinations are satisfactory. British brands of wool are marked B, American brands A. The left column denotes the fabric; the right, the kind of wool suitable.

CLOSELY WOVEN FABRICS	FINE SOFT WOOLLEN YARN
Plain casement cloth	A. "Single-Twist" or homespun
Mohair casement cloth	Fine scarf yarn
Organdie	Fabric yarns
Spun silk	Shetland
Mercerized cloths	Saxony
Medium weight linens	French zephyr
Cotton crêpes	Lustre Iceland
Fine nets	
	B. Fine spun wools
	Two-ply Shetland wool
	Angora
	Viyella

PLATE XXI

Crewel embroidery used for decorative hangings

MEDIUM WEIGHT FABRICS

Plain tapestry cloth
Antique cloth
Dyed cotton flannel
Homespun
Monk's cloth or sand serge
Terry cloth or towelling
British crash
Rep

MEDIUM YARNS

A. Minerva
   Medium Bear brand
   Crewel wools
   Coverlet yarn
   Homespun
   Zephyr
   Spanish yarn
   Tapestry wool
   Germantown zephyr

B. Three-ply knitting yarn
   Shetland
   Medium Angora
   Medium crochet wool

MESH MATERIALS

Theatrical gauze
Loose nets

MEDIUM AND FLUFFY YARNS

A. Lustro
   Heavy scarf yarn
   Coverlet yarn
   Zephyr
   Fine Shetland
   French zephyr
   Floss

B. Fine spun Angora
   Sirdar crochet wool
   Beehive Angora
   Viyella knitting yarn

FELT AND OILCLOTH

MEDIUM CLOSELY SPUN WOOLS

A. Minerva
   Medium Bear brand
   Zephyr
   Belspun
   Spanish stocking yarn

FELT AND OILCLOTH
(*contd.*)

B. Medium weight yarns of firm
    twist
  Tapestry wools
  White Heather zephyr
  White Heather embroidery
    wool

COARSE MATERIALS

Burlap
Matting
Coarse linen
Stiff fibre nets
Burlap hessian

HEAVY YARNS

A. Heavy Bear brand
  Blanket yarn
  Germantown
  Rug wool
  Sultana
  Scotch

B. Filgora yarns
  Furida yarns
  Turkey rug wool
  Persian rug wool
  Baltic rug wool

COLOUR SCHEMES. Two things determine the success
of woolcraft creations: their design and the colours
chosen for background and ornament. With the right
colour balance, the textile background will bring out
the woollen embroidery with vivid beauty. It is worth
while spending a little time in planning colour schemes.
Following are some suggestions. The first colour of
each group is best suited for the background, although,
of course, the colours are interchangeable for individual
needs.

GREEN

Green, plum colour, touches of yellow.
Green, grey, black accents.
Light green, bottle green.
Soft green, heliotrope, buff.
Green, rust, or henna.

Green, oyster white, or cream.
Pale green, coral, blue.
Drab green, *tête de negre*.
Nile green, orchid.
Peacock green, apricot, sand.
Pistache, tan.
Pea-green, grey, yellow, salmon.
Green, grey, red, touches of black.
Green, gold, henna, blue.
Pale green, orange, yellow, henna, brown.
Chartreuse, mauve, blue, rose.

BLUE.

Blue combines singly with peach, apricot, grey, black, cream, yellow, orange, and white.
Blue, biscuit colour, orange.
Blue, cream, plum.
Pale blue, dark blue, white.
Peacock blue, *naturelle*.
Blue, green, ivory.
Turquoise, sand, henna, green.
Turquoise, henna.
Blue, mauve, rose.
Steel blue, brown, white.

PURPLE.

Deep purple, soft pale green, maize.
Egg-plant, peach.
Raspberry, maize.
Purple, grey, green.
Orchid, ivory.
Lavender, corn colour.

CREAM AND WHITE.

Cream combines singly with any colour except grey, orange and yellow.
Cream, rose, apricot, *jaune*.
Cream, orange, black.
Faded cream, coral, deep blue.

Naturelle, green, henna.
Naturelle, soft blue, orange.
Sand, rust, blue.
White, sea-green, blue.
Ivory, orchid.
Ivory, black or brown or blue or purple.
Beige, brown.

YELLOW.

Yellow combines singly with brown, black, green, purple
blue, red.
Maize, blue, green, black.
Corn colour, purple.
Lemon, olive.
Yellow, plum, grey.
Yellow, blue, black.
Yellow, green, orange, flame, black.
Yellow, orange, brown, henna.

BROWN.

Brown combines singly with yellow, orange, cream, white,
flesh, apricot, ecru, pale blue, pale green.
Brown, coral, tan.
Brown, yellow, orange.
Brown, tan, flame.

RED.

Red combines singly with white, black, pale blue, green,
yellow, grey.
Red, pale green, grey, yellow.
Rose, pale green, silver-grey.
Cedar, blue, henna, corn, green.
Henna, green.
Soft pink, pale blue.
Soft pink, deep rose.
Soft pink, brown, white.
Terra-cotta, reseda, old white.
Lacquer, yellow.
Copper, beige or cream.

GREY, BLACK, WHITE.

Grey, black, white.
Grey, rose, green.
Grey, red, black.
Grey, black, green, yellow.
Putty, yellow.
Black combines with white, green, light blue, red, tan, yellow, orange, and orchid.
White combines with any colour.

PLATE XXII

Delightful mushrooms colourfully stitched on natural
background.

Designed by Pera Lee